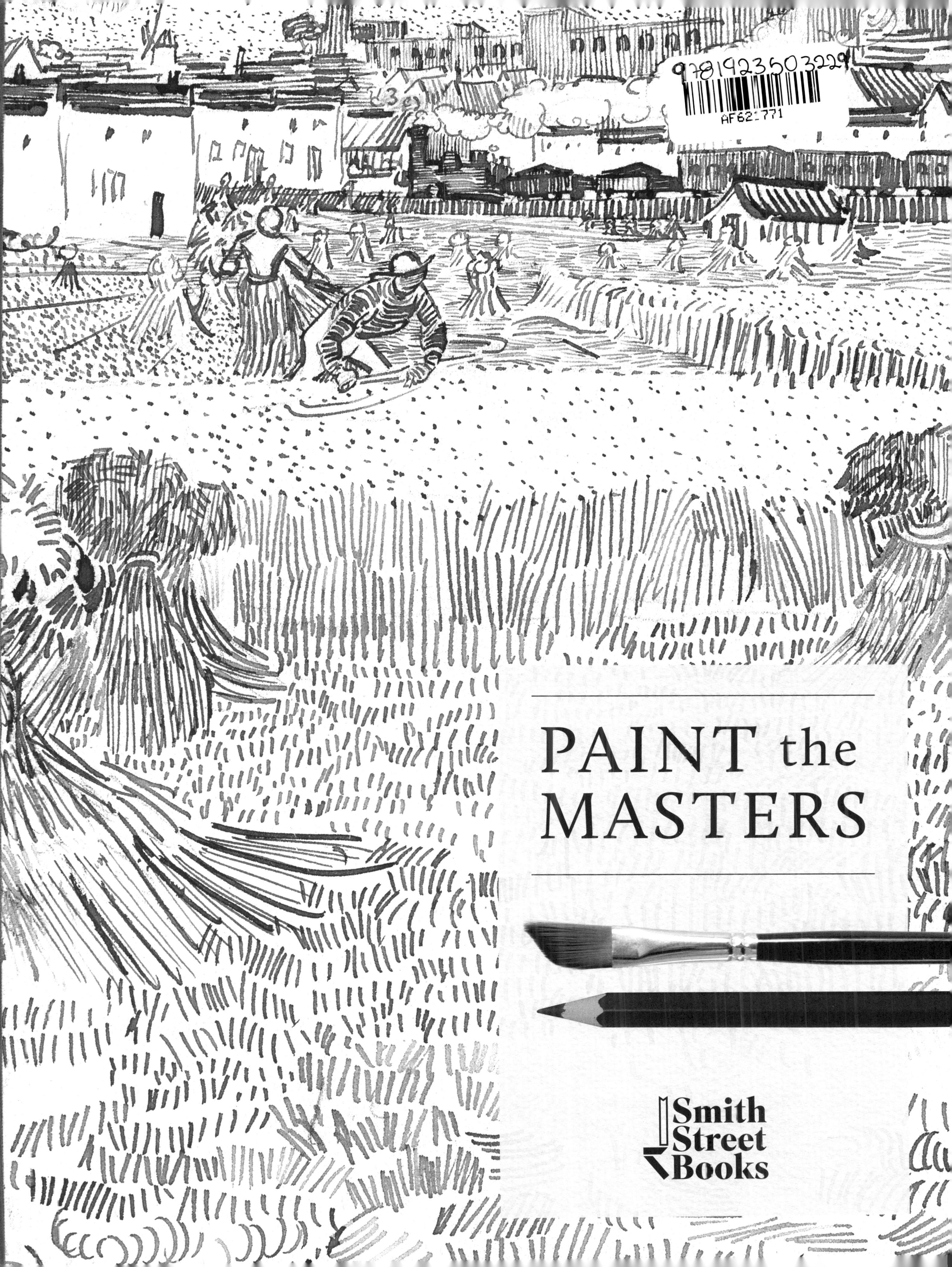

# PAINT the MASTERS

Smith Street Books

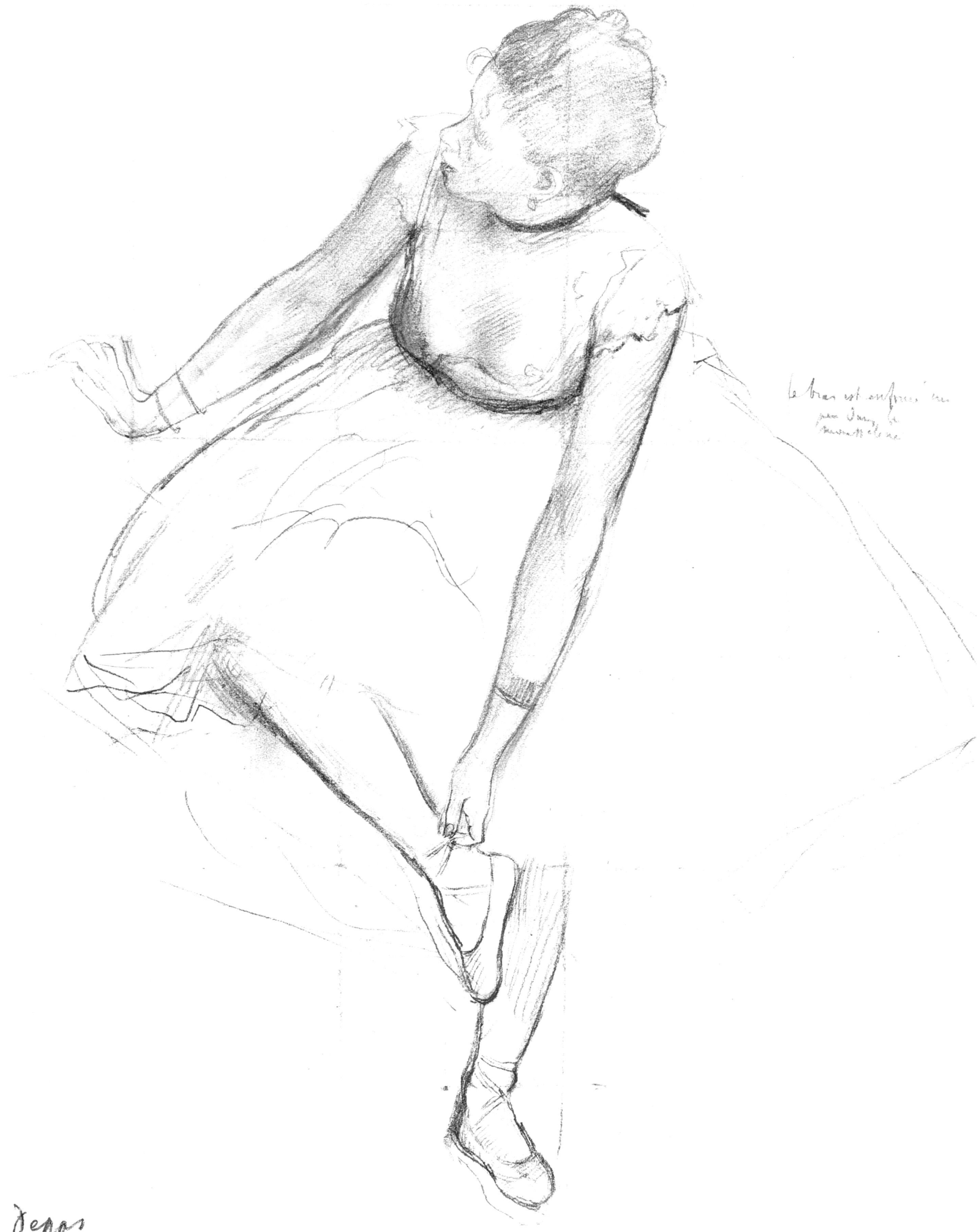
Degas

# EDGAR DEGAS

1834–1917

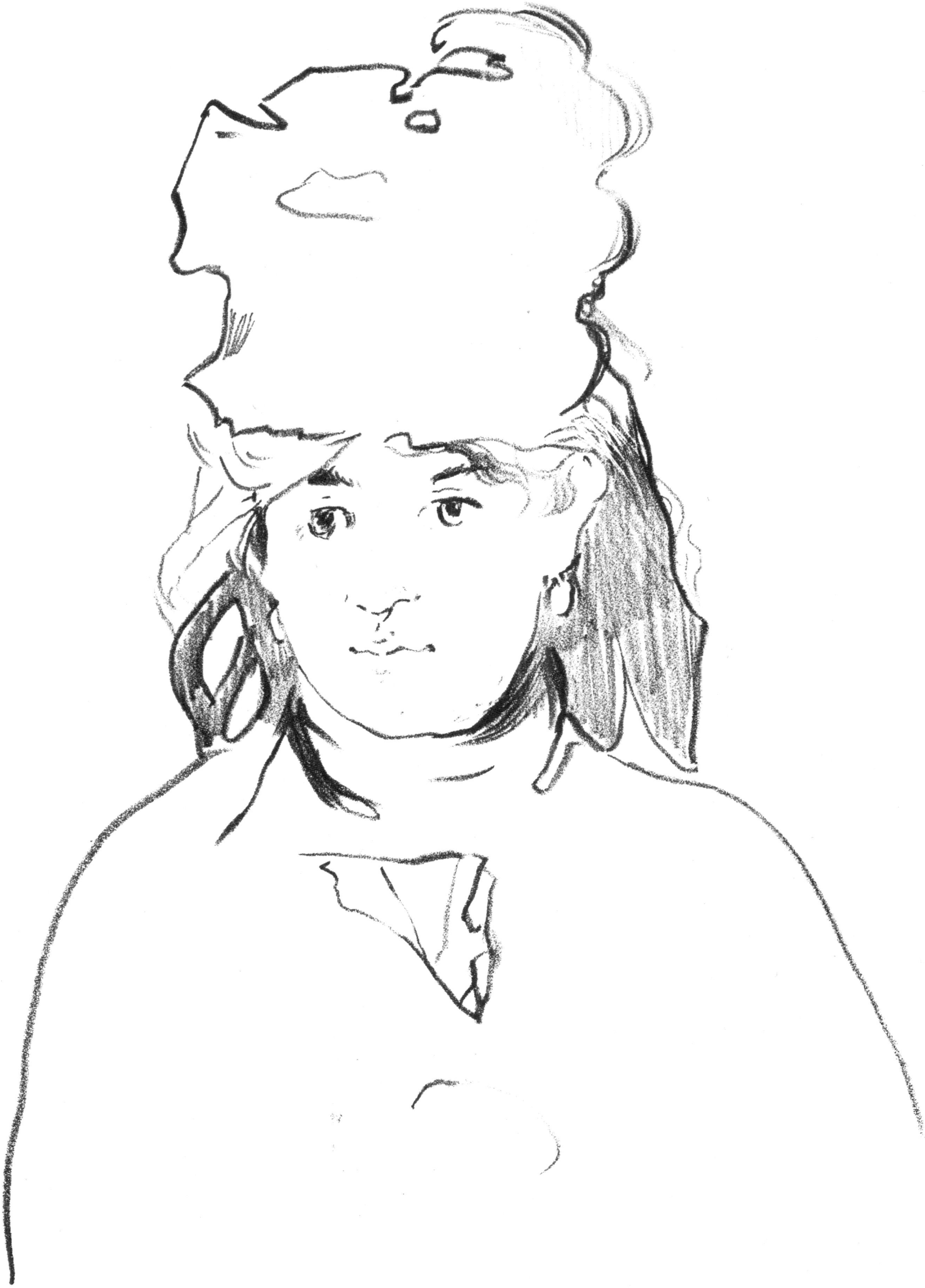

# ÉDOUARD MANET

1832–1883

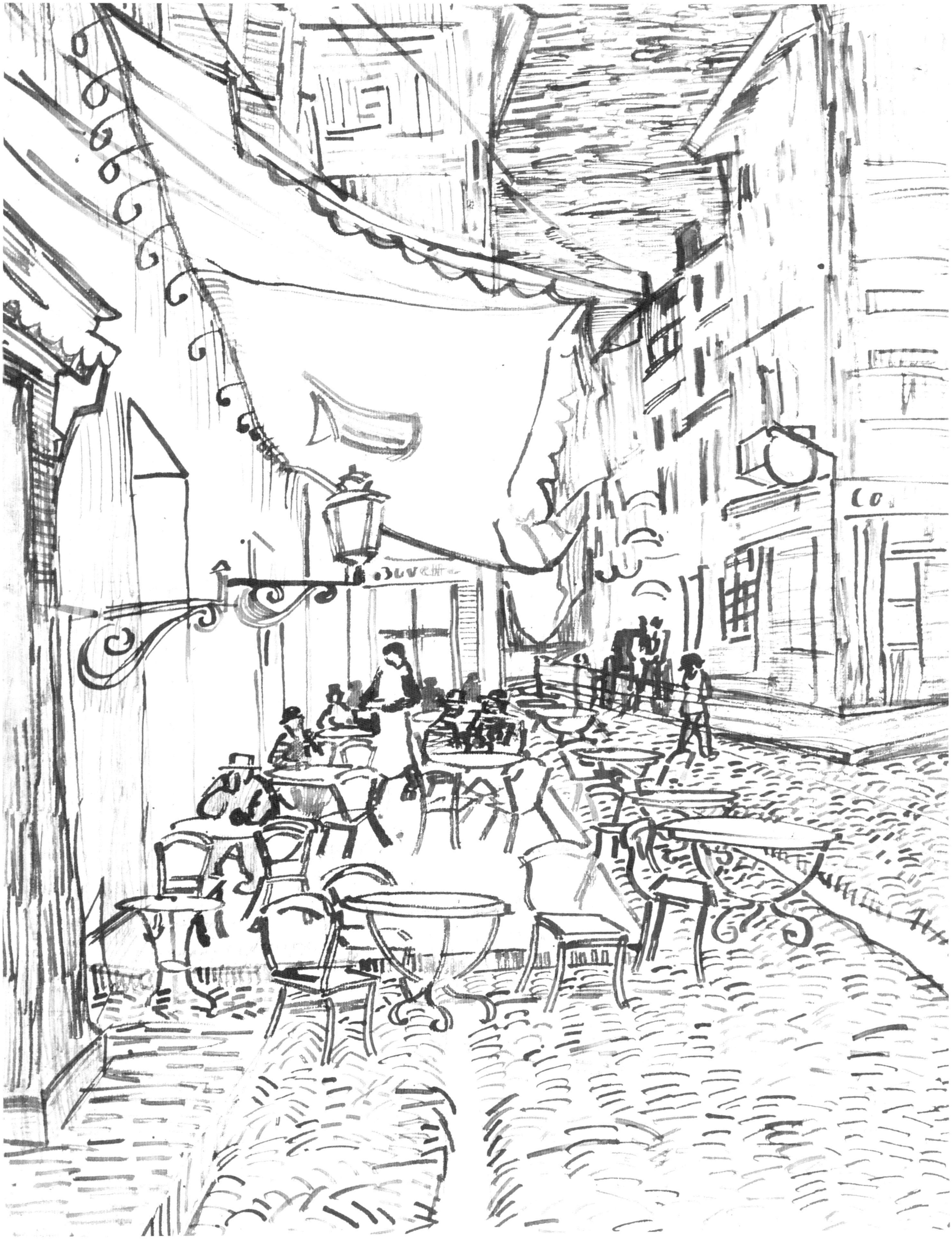

# VINCENT
# van GOGH

1853–1890

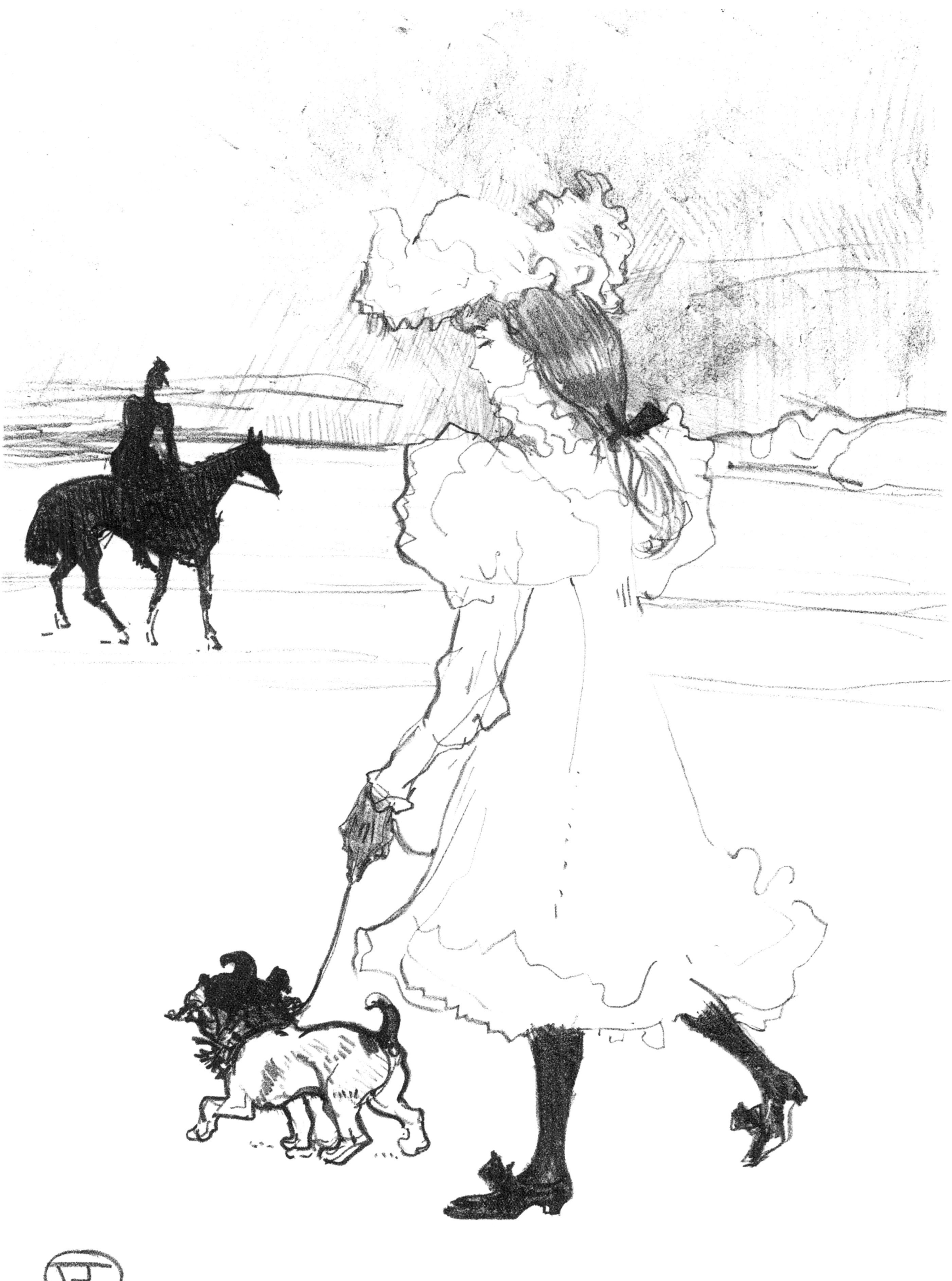

# HENRI de TOULOUSE-LAUTREC

1864–1901

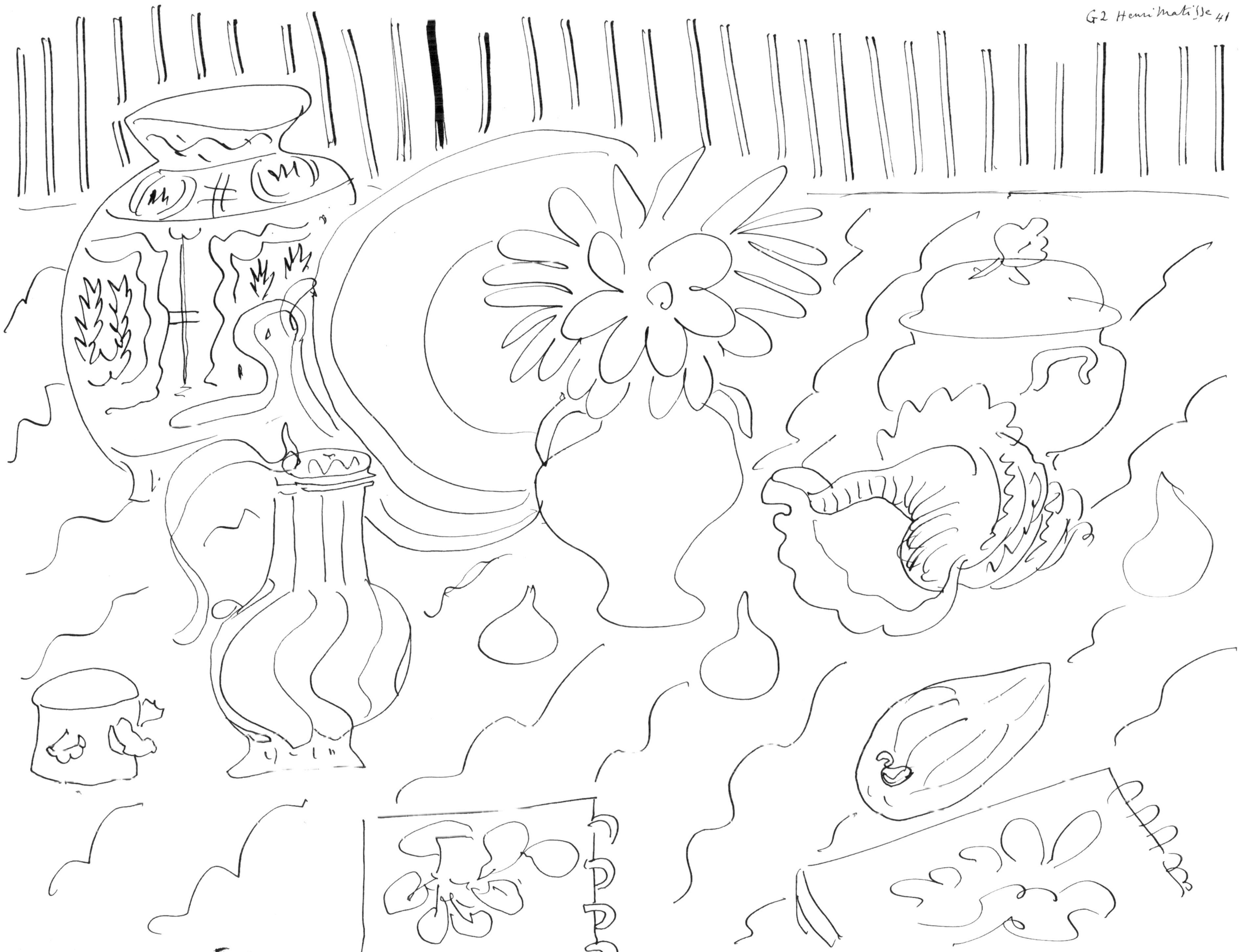
G2 Henri Matisse 41

# HENRI MATISSE

1869–1954

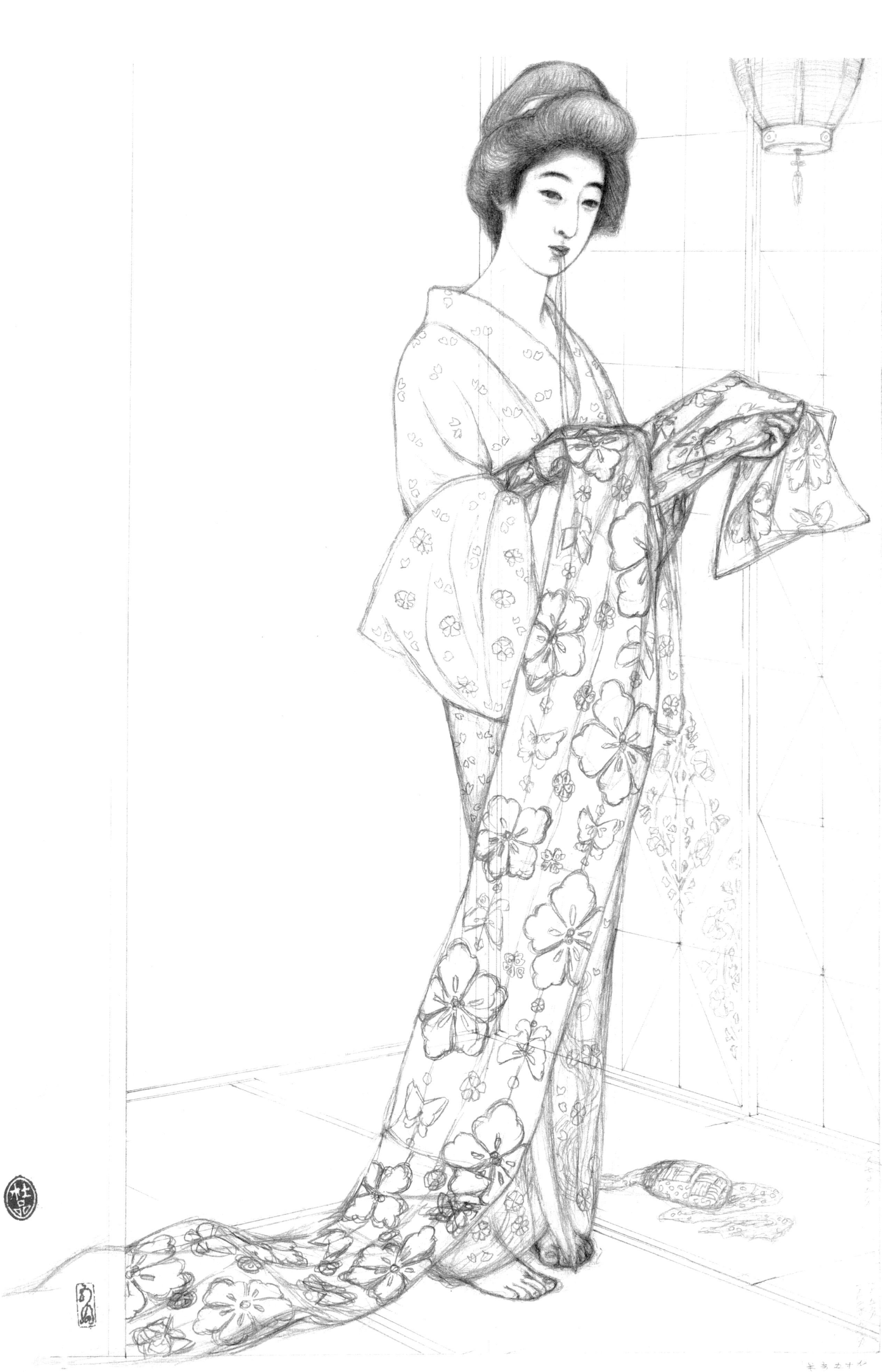

# GOYŌ HASHIGUCHI

1880–1921

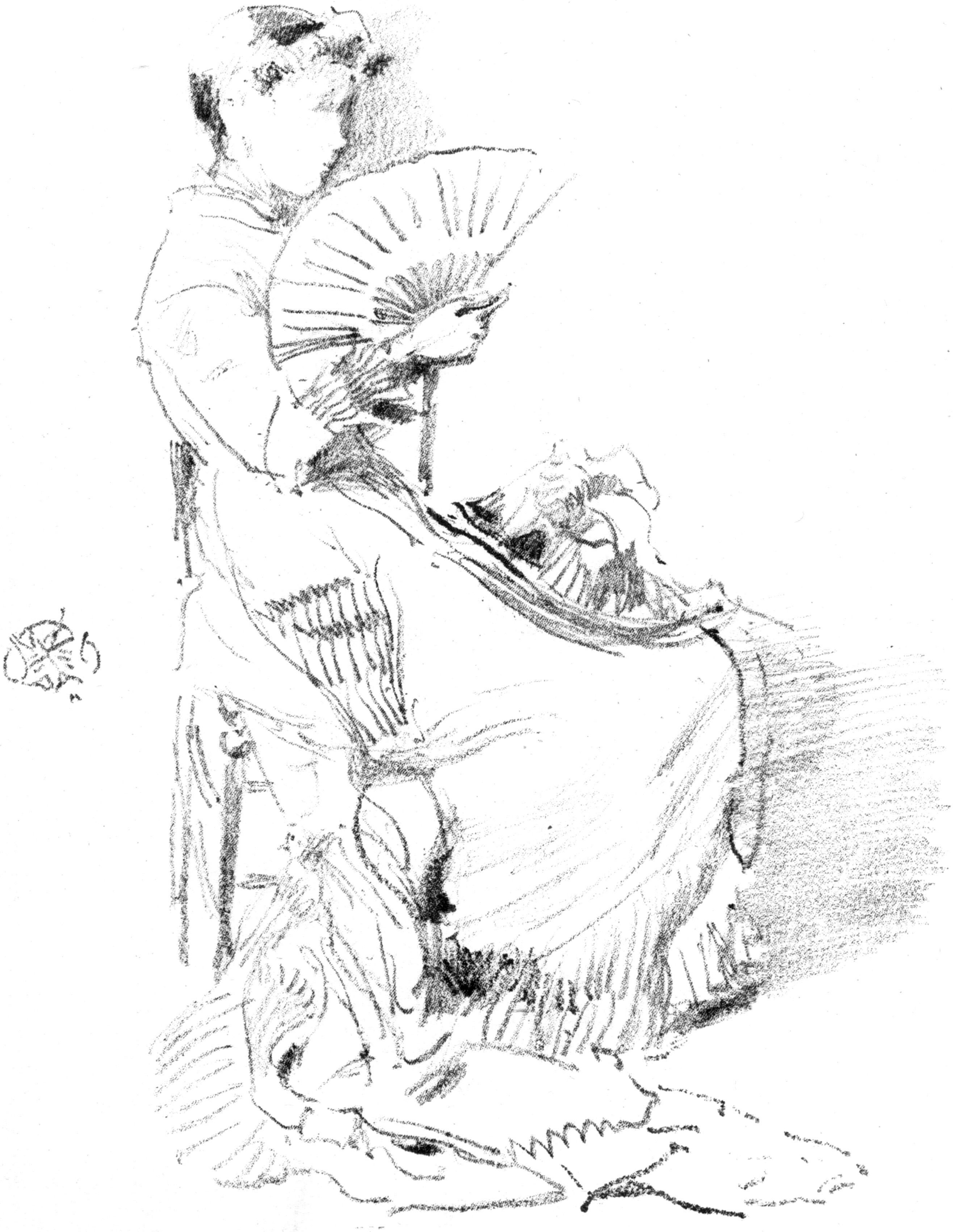

# JAMES McNEILL WHISTLER

1834–1903

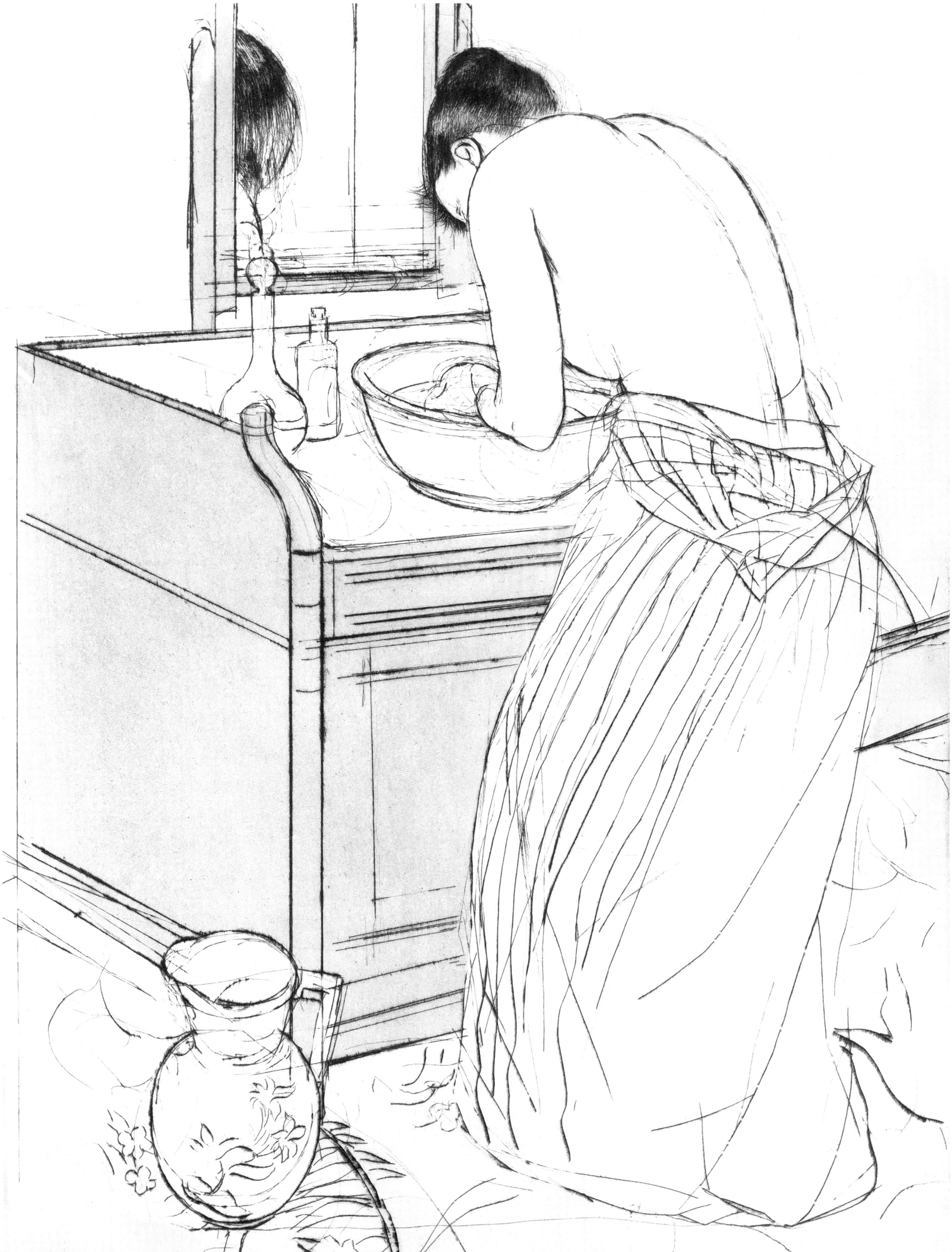

# MARY CASSATT

1844–1926

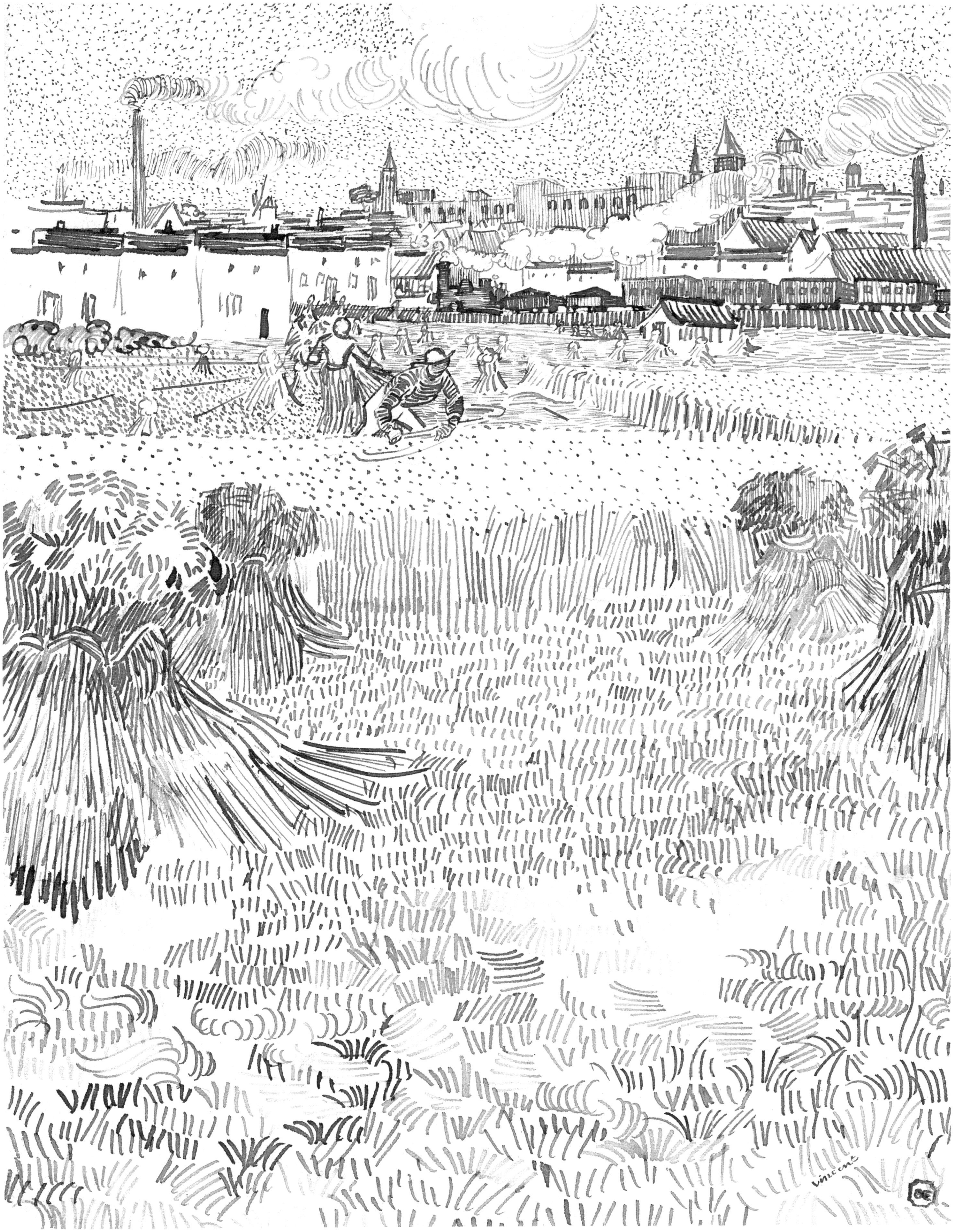
Vincent

# VINCENT van GOGH

1853–1890

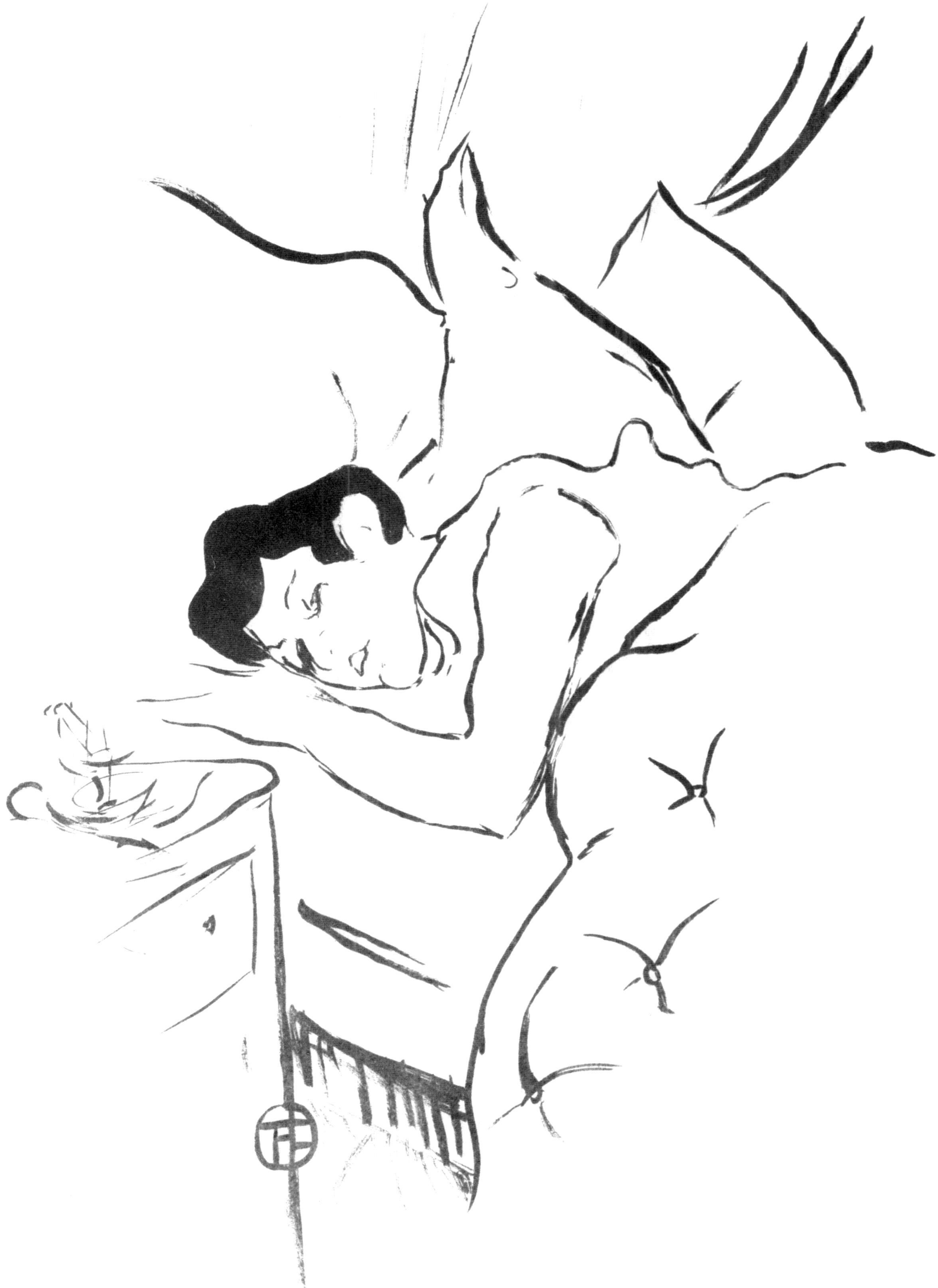

Nº 14

T-Lautrec

# HENRI de TOULOUSE-LAUTREC

1864–1901

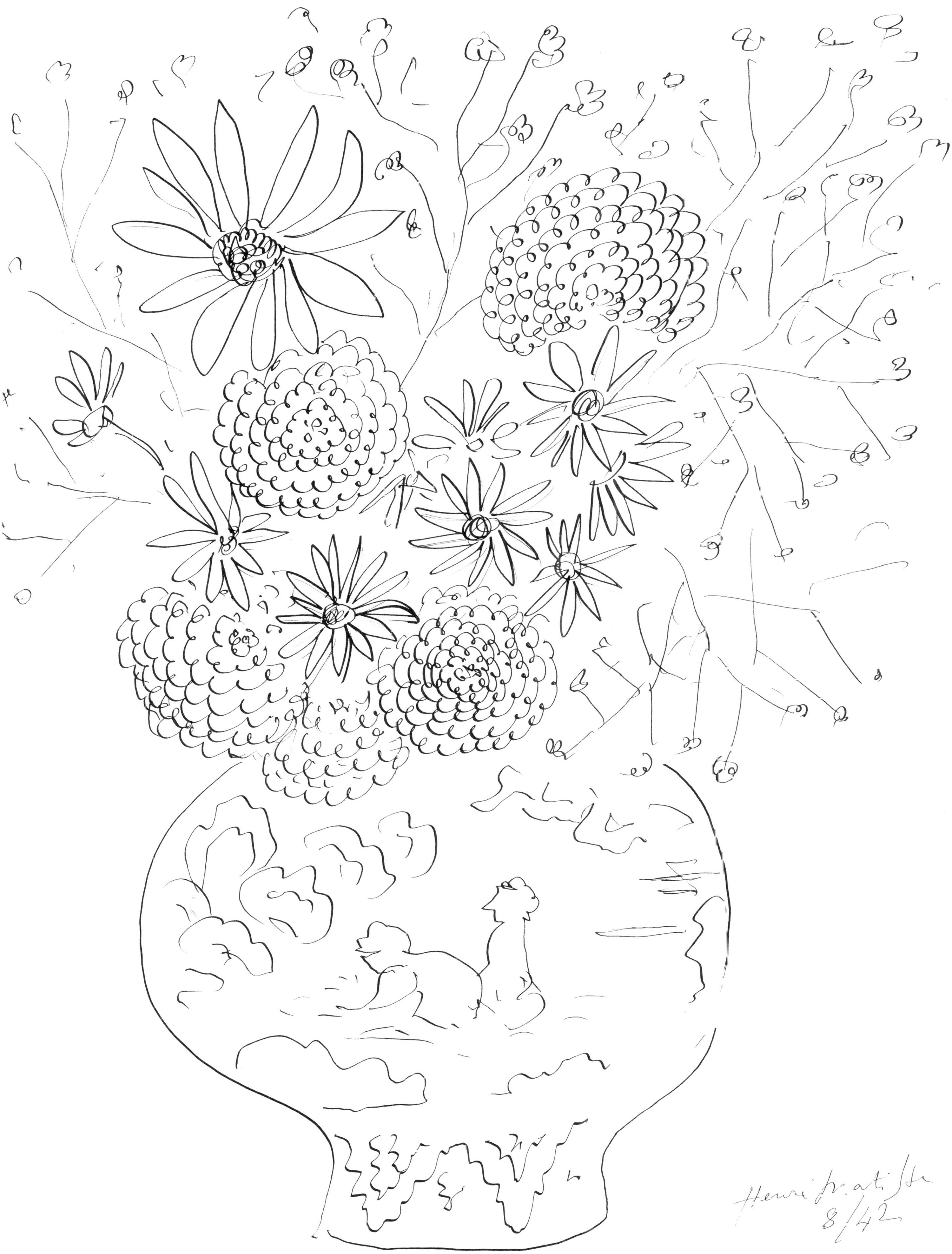
Henri Matisse
8/42

# HENRI MATISSE

1869–1954

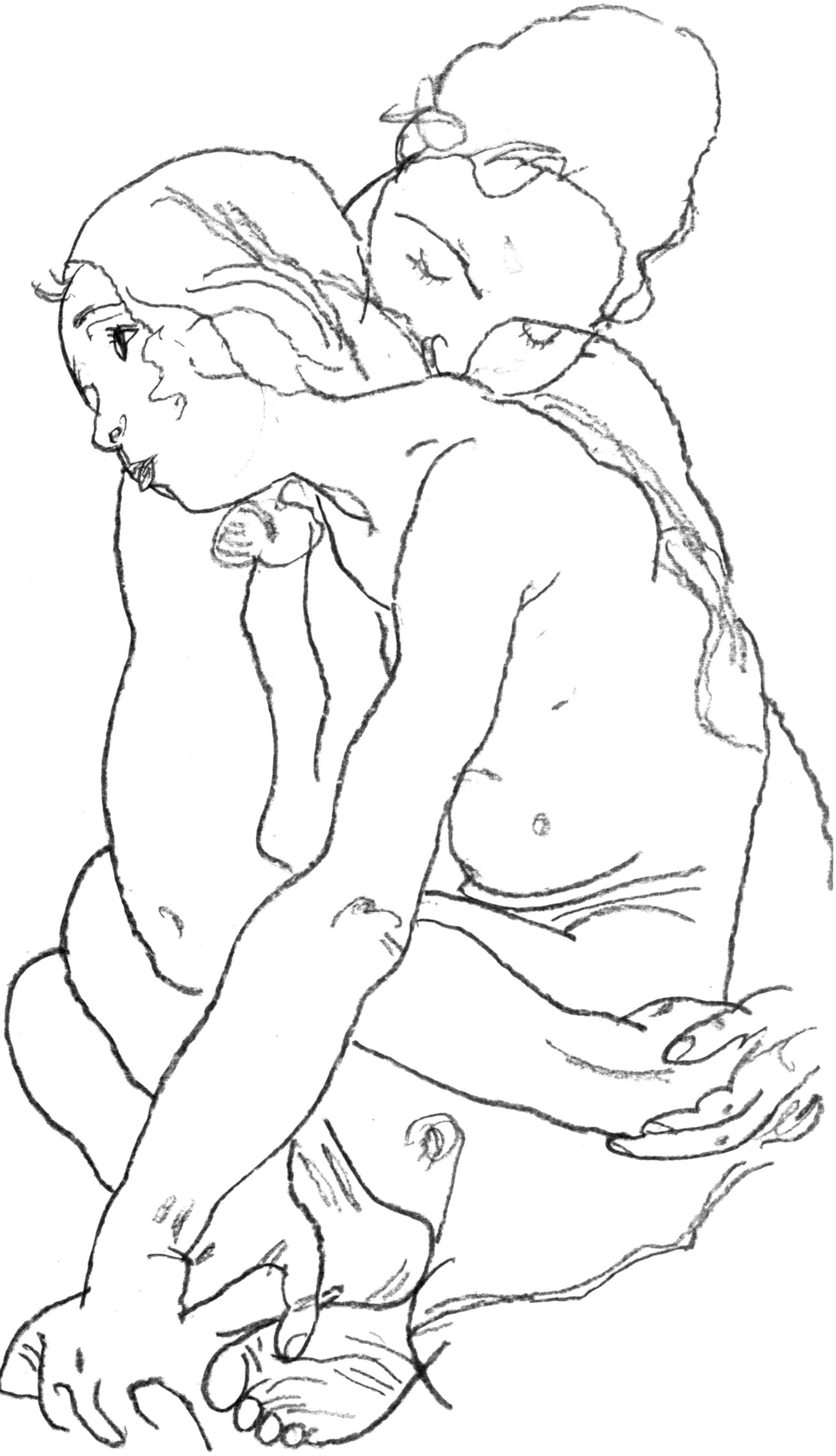
EGON SCHIELE 1918

# EGON SCHIELE

1890–1918

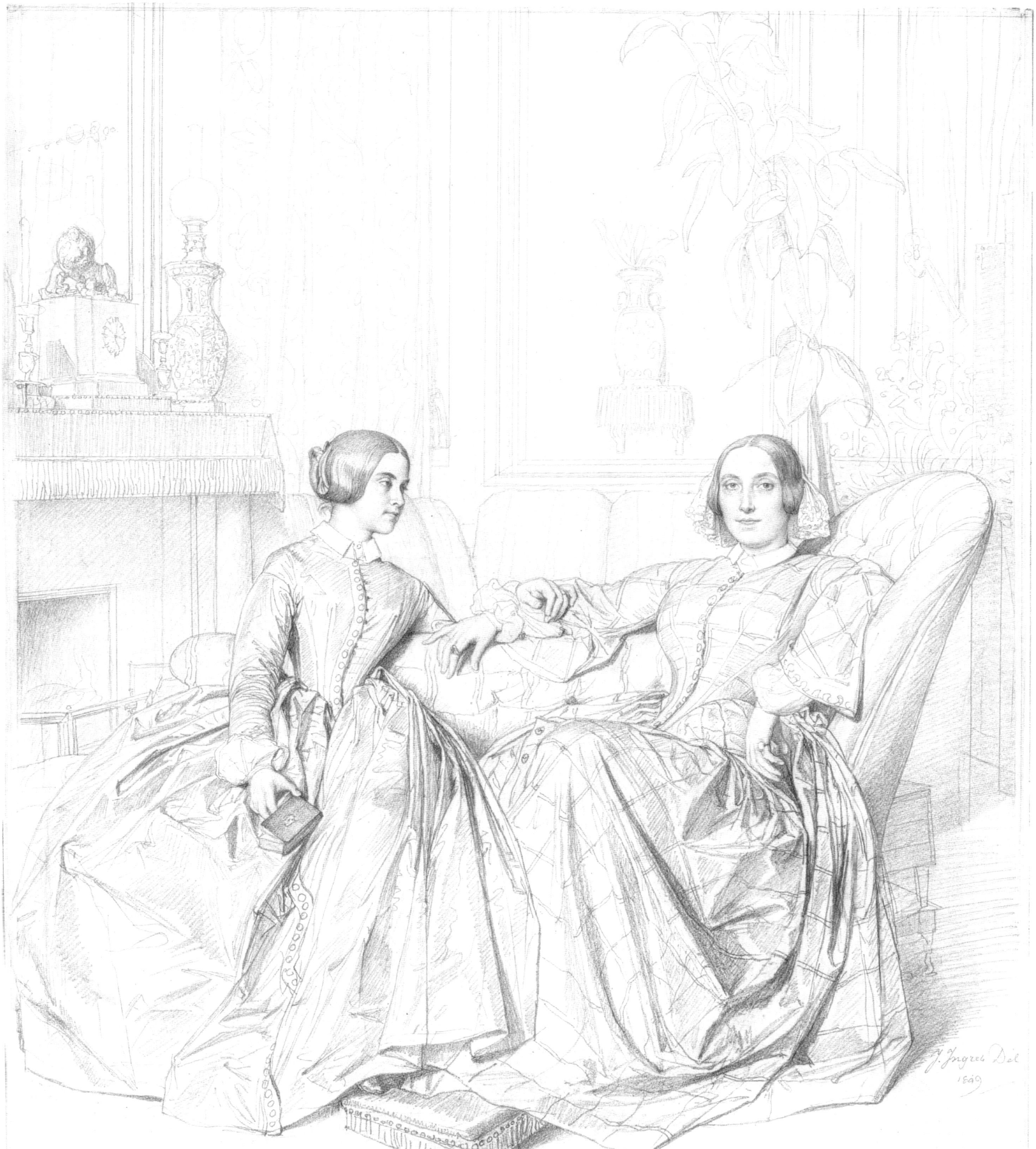
J. Ingres Del
1849

# JEAN-AUGUSTE-DOMINIQUE INGRES

1780–1867

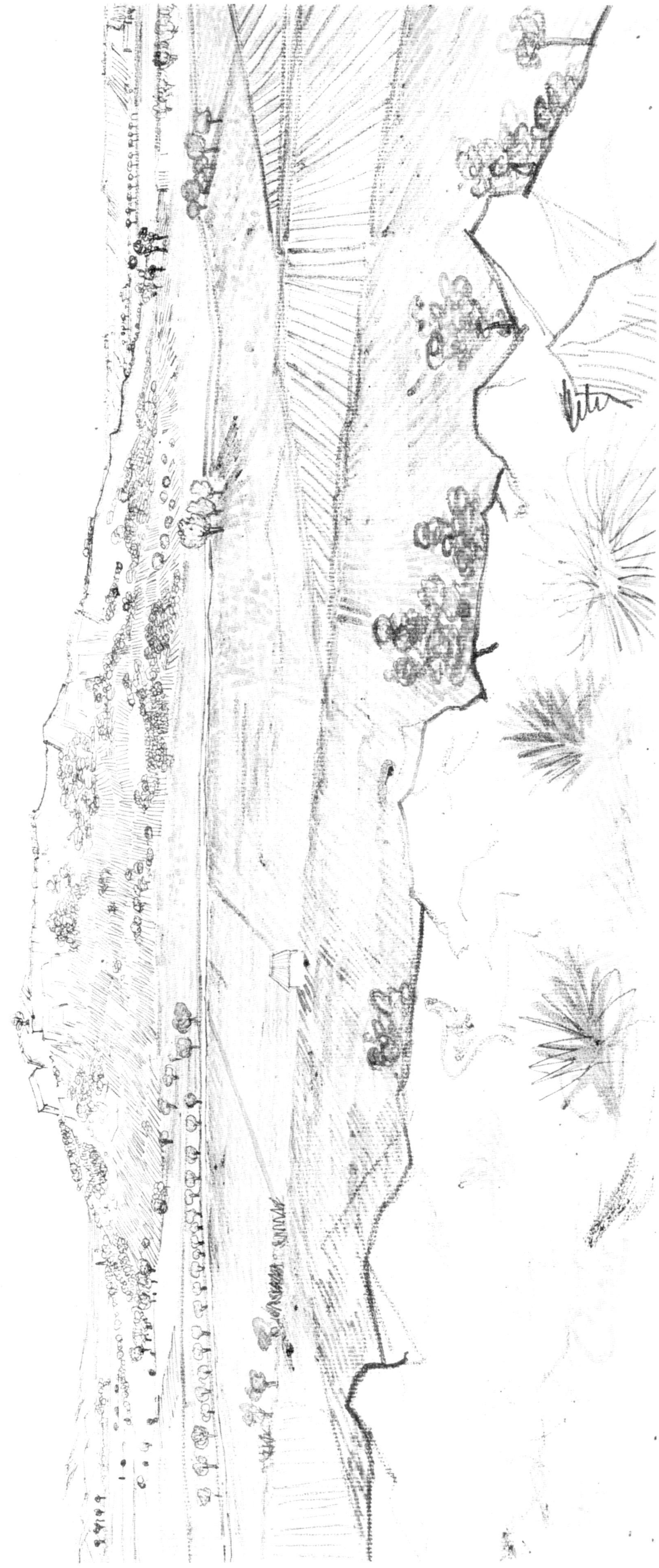

# VINCENT van GOGH

1853–1890

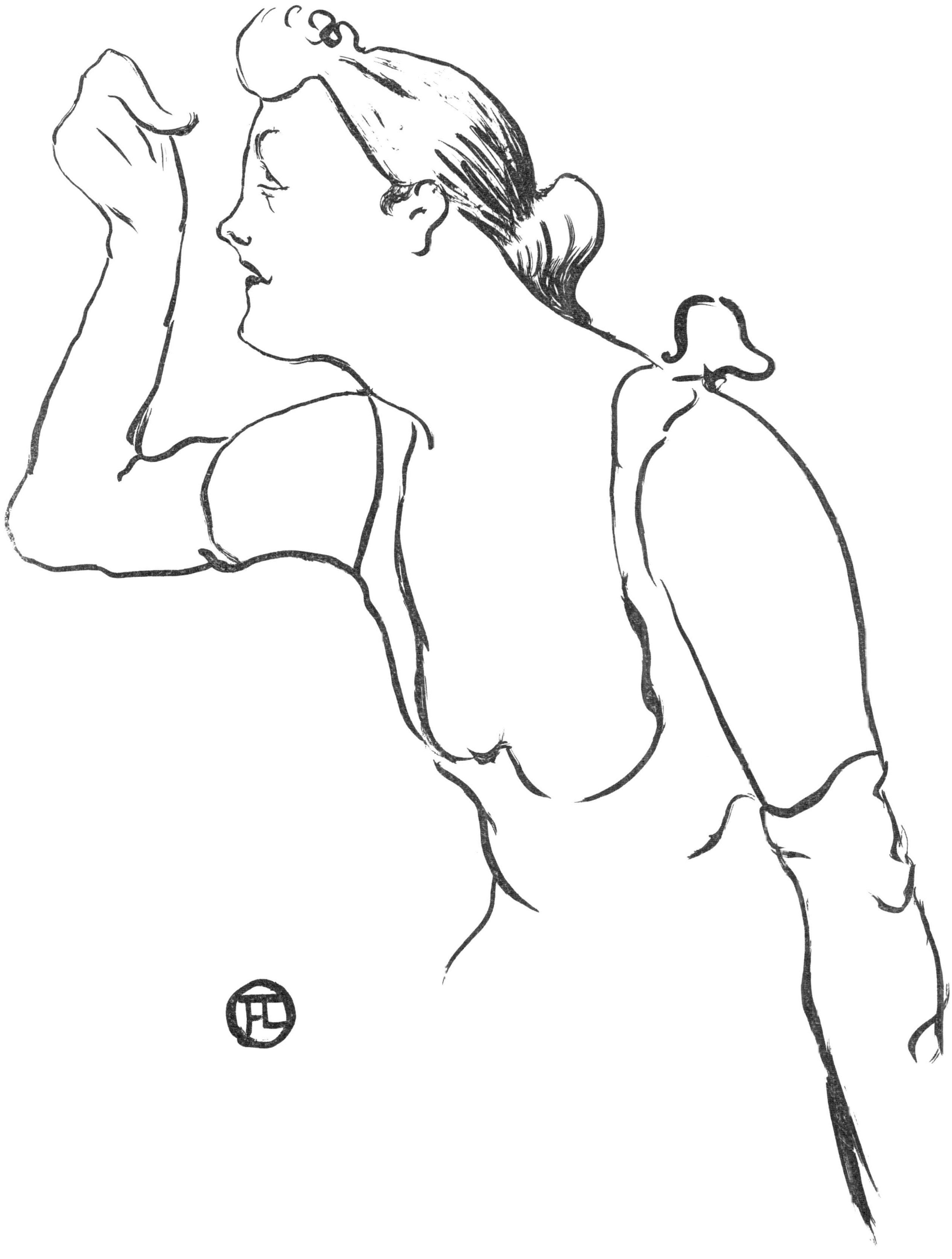

# HENRI de TOULOUSE-LAUTREC

1864–1901

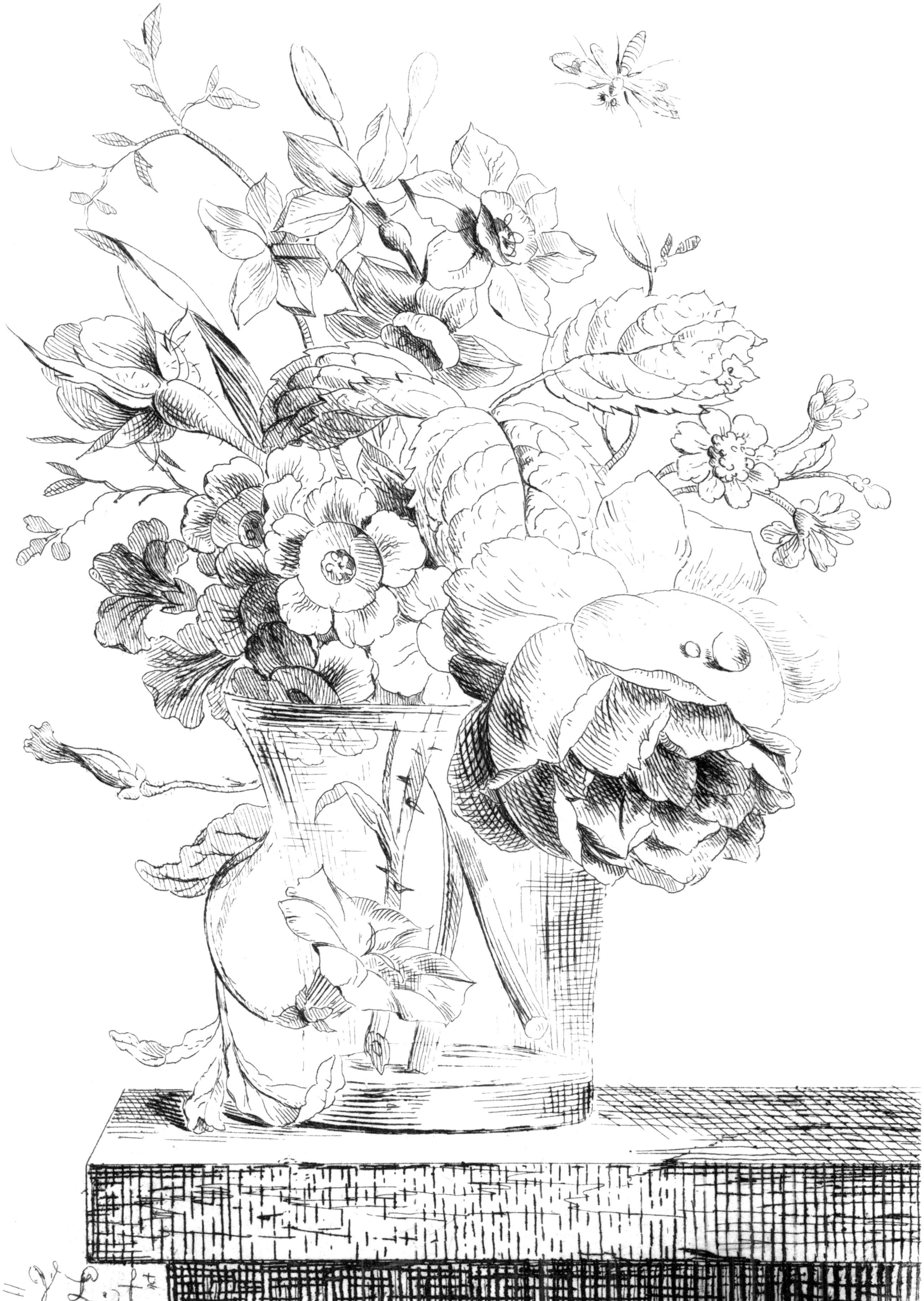

# WILLEM van LEEN

1753–1825

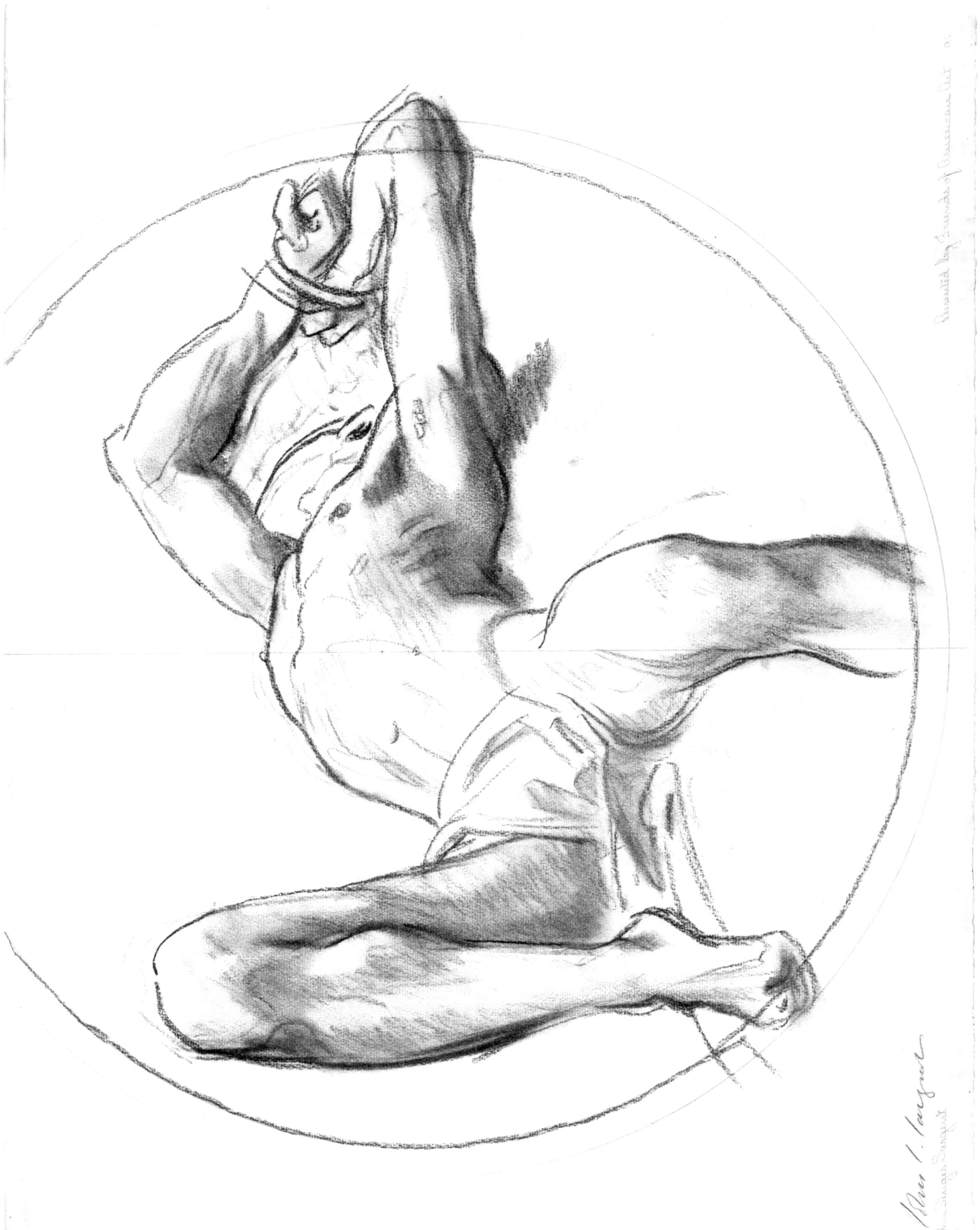

# JOHN SINGER SARGENT

1856–1925

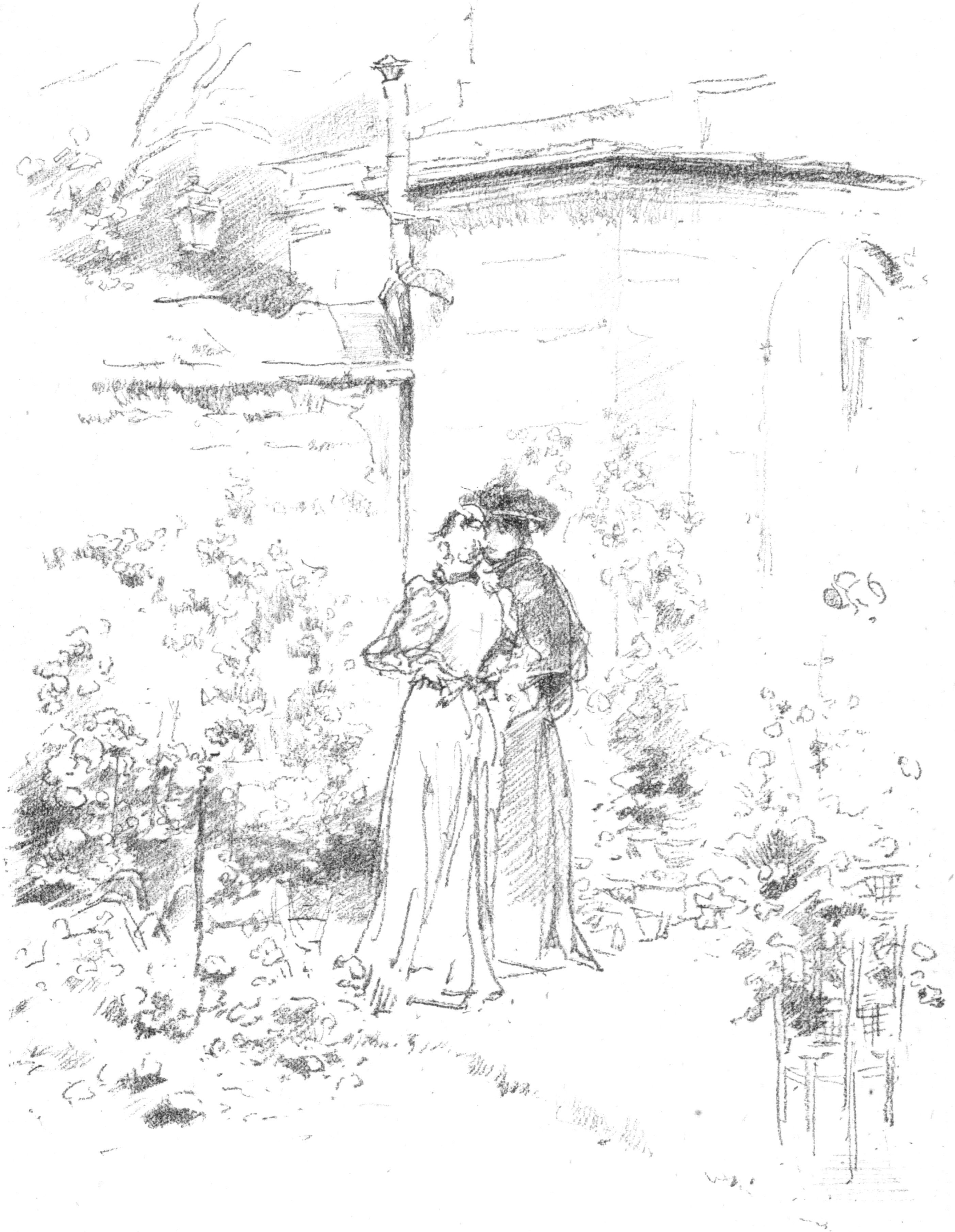

# JAMES McNEILL WHISTLER

1834–1903

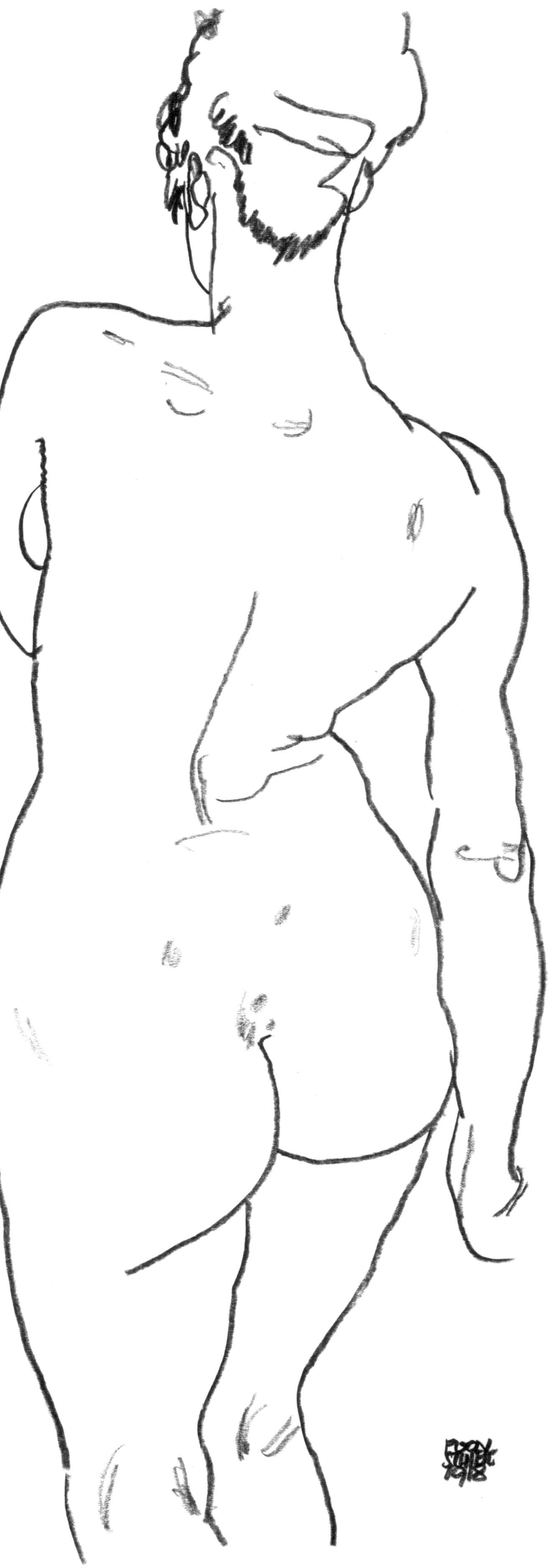
EGON
SCHIELE
1918

# EGON SCHIELE

1890–1918

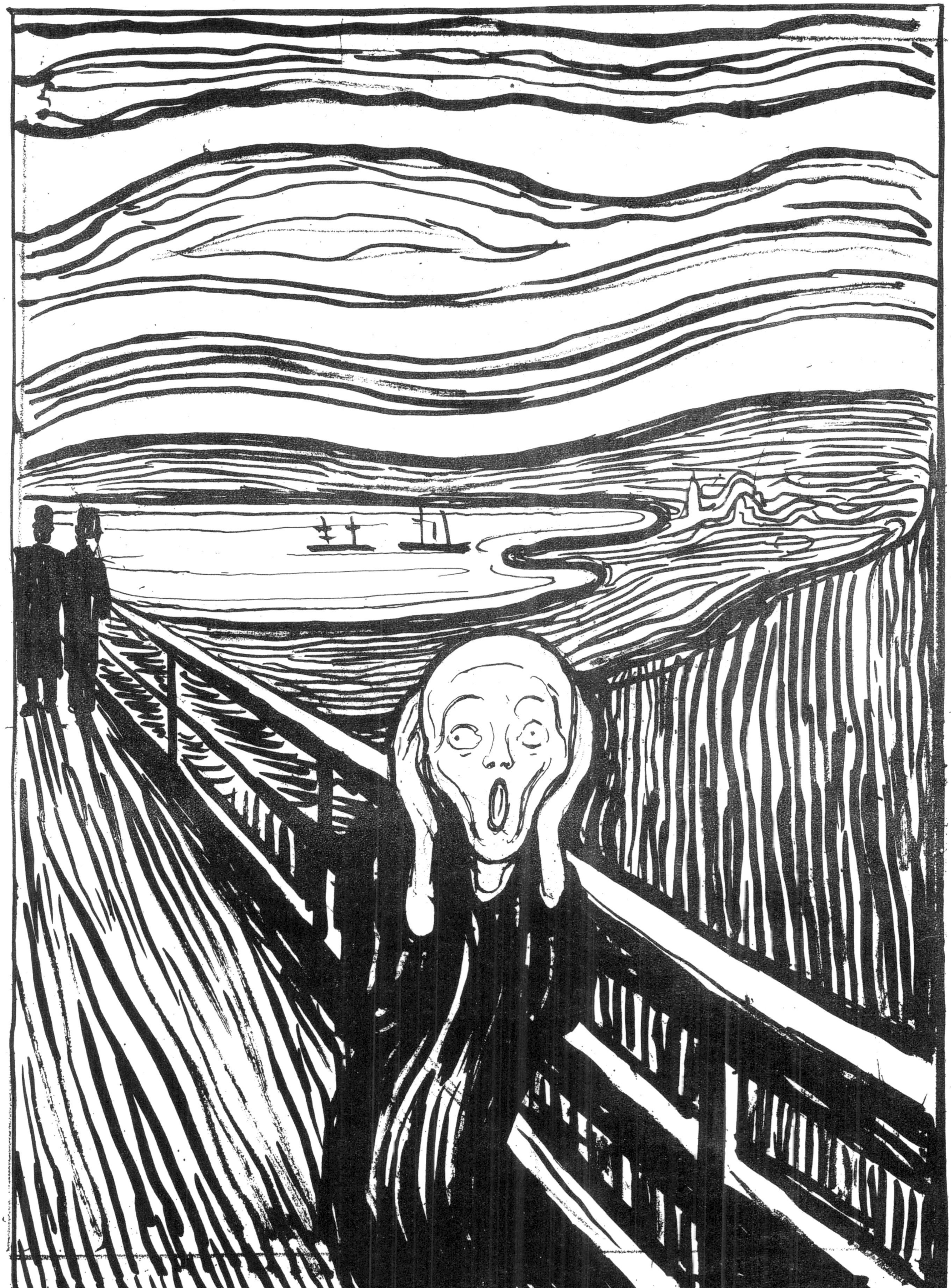

# EDVARD MUNCH

1863–1944

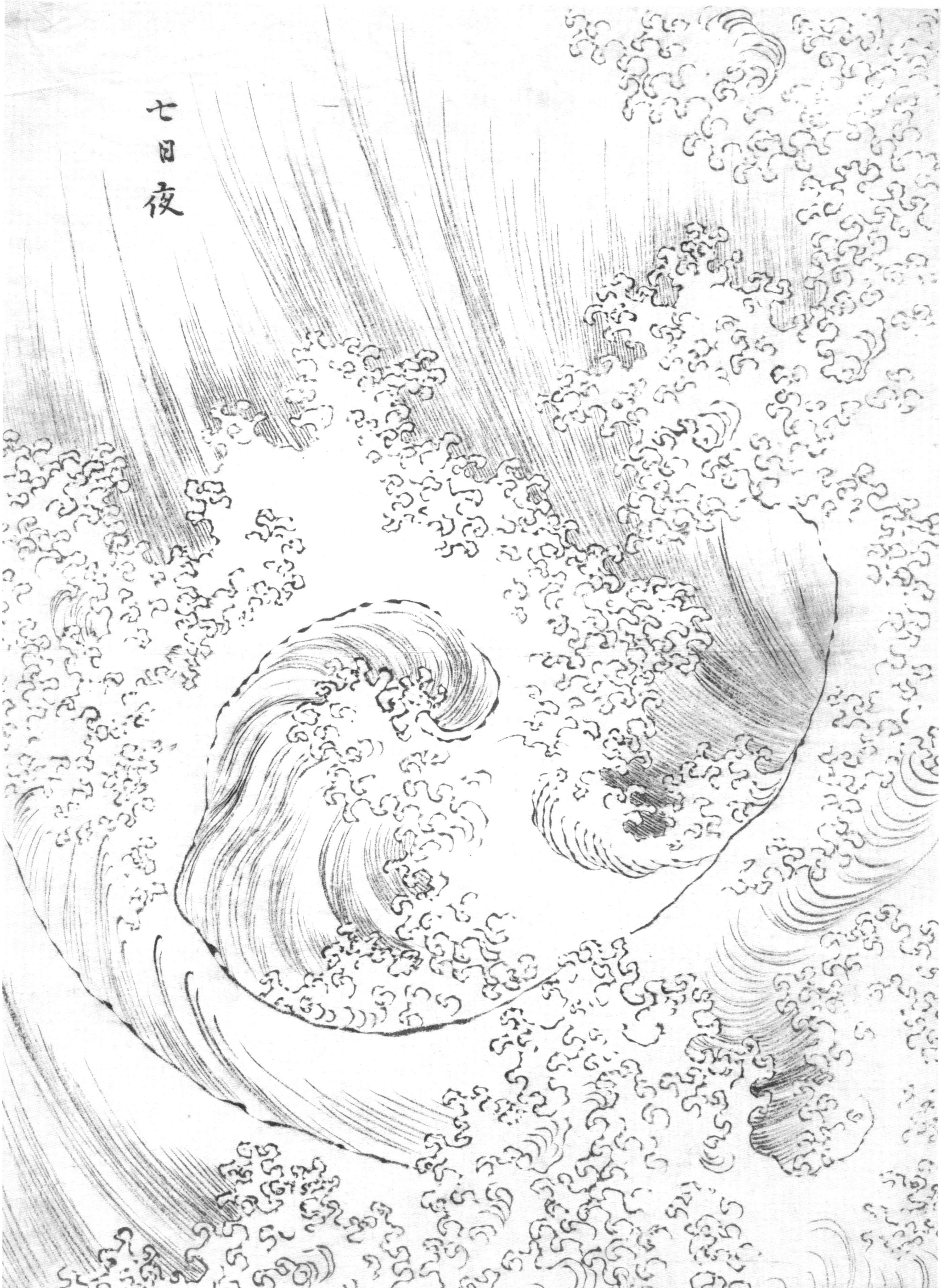
七日夜

# KATSUSHIKA HOKUSAI

1760–1849

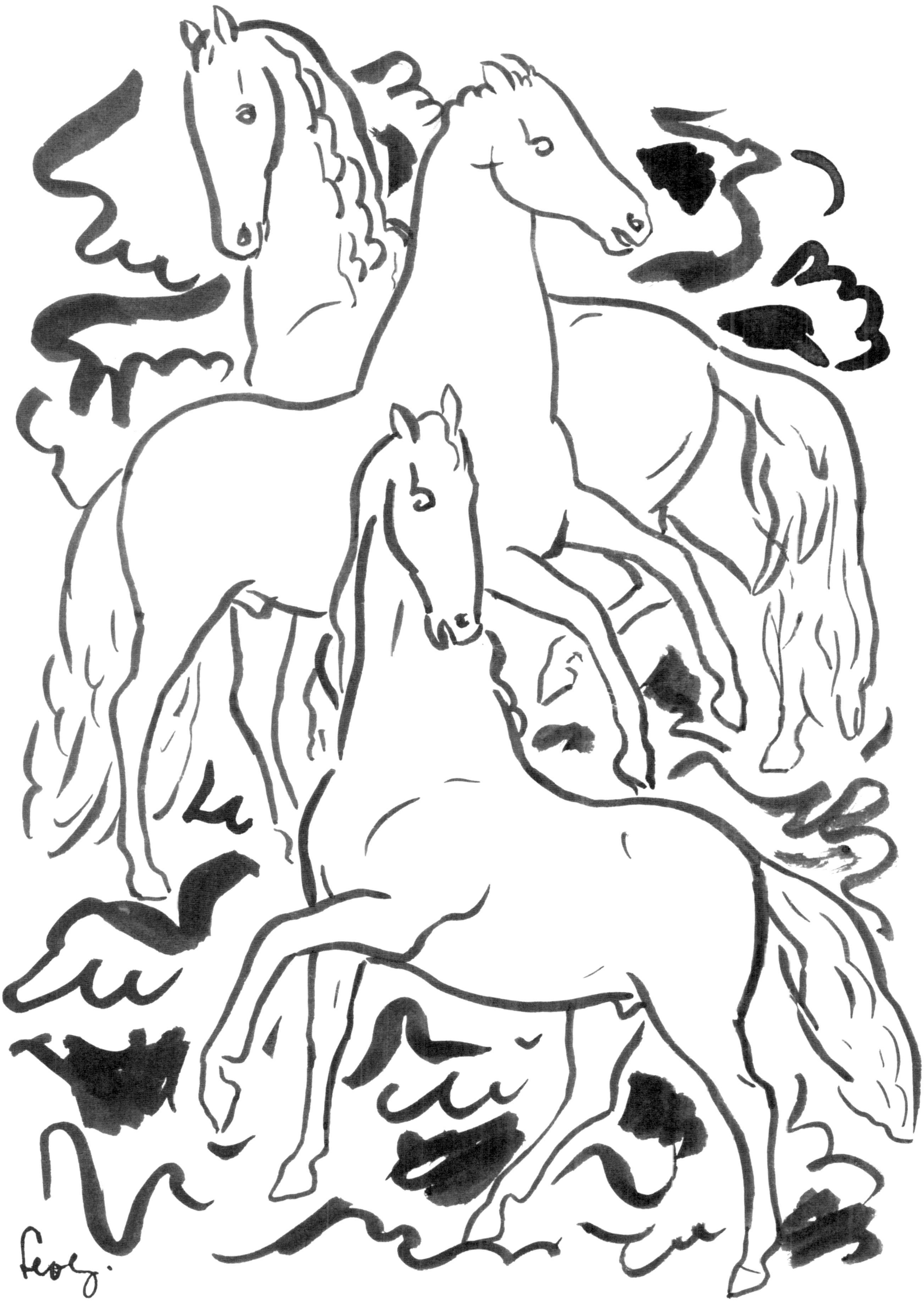

# LEO GESTEL

1881–1941

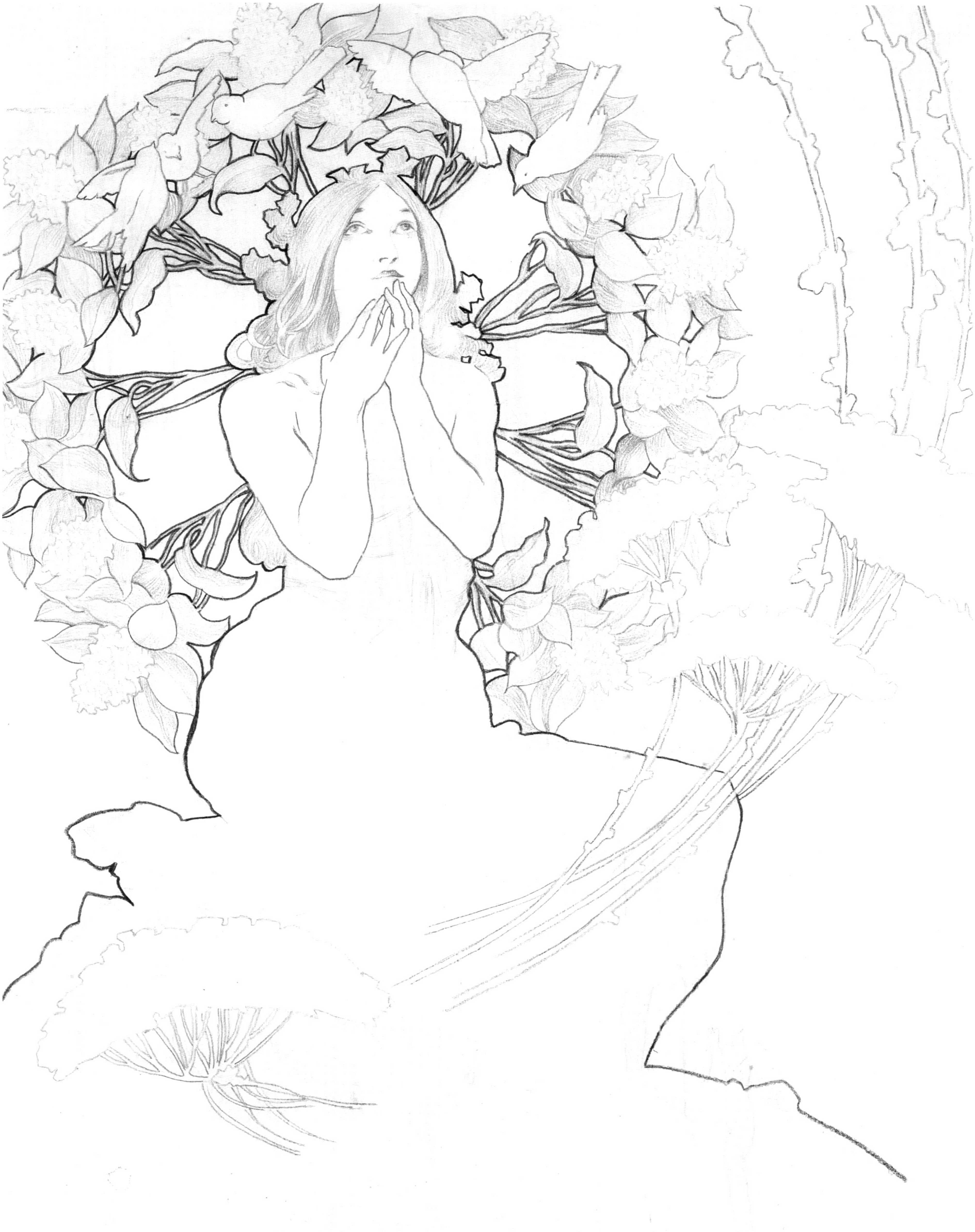

# ALPHONSE MUCHA

1860–1939

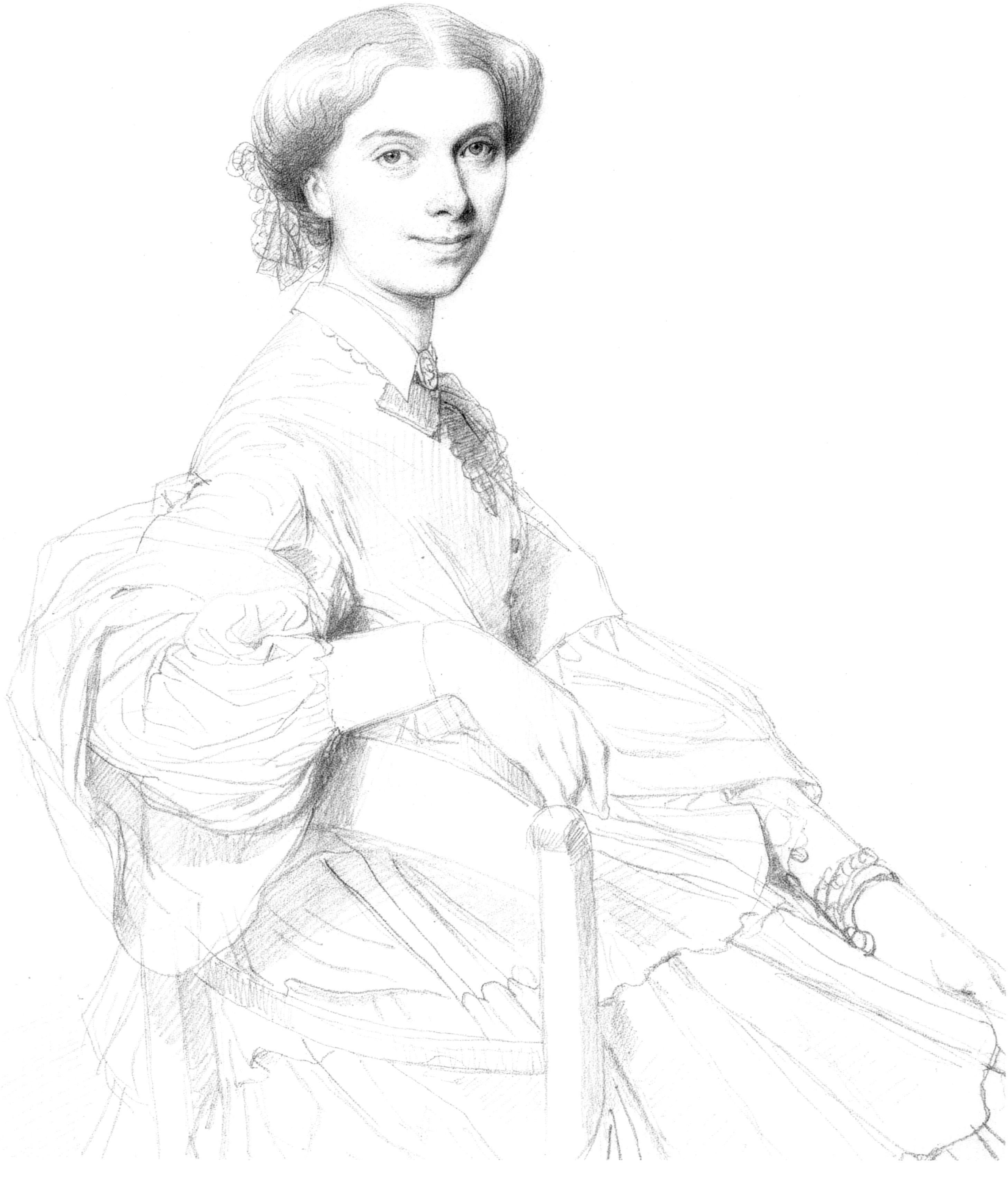

# JEAN-AUGUSTE-DOMINIQUE INGRES

1780–1867

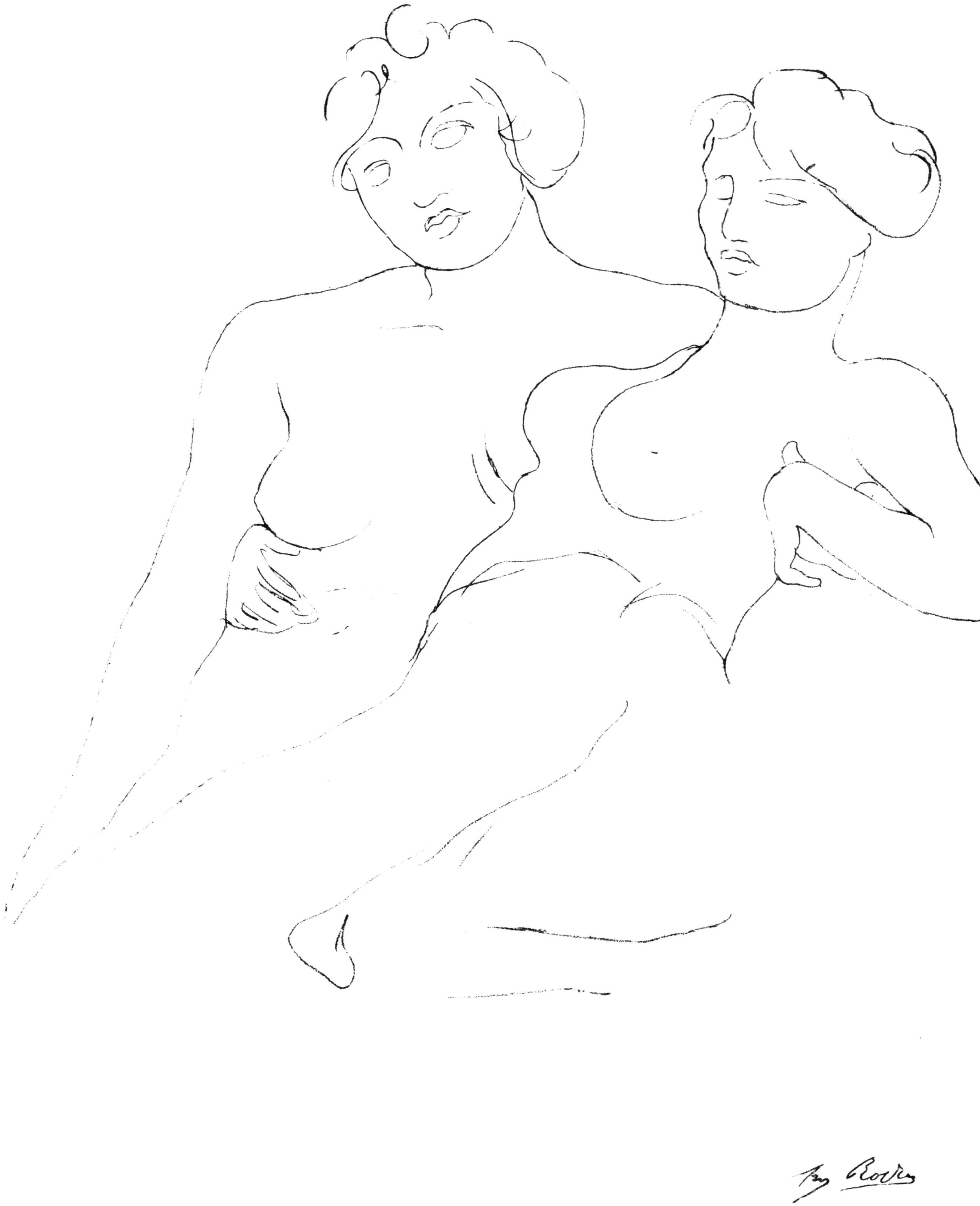

# AUGUSTE RODIN

1840–1917

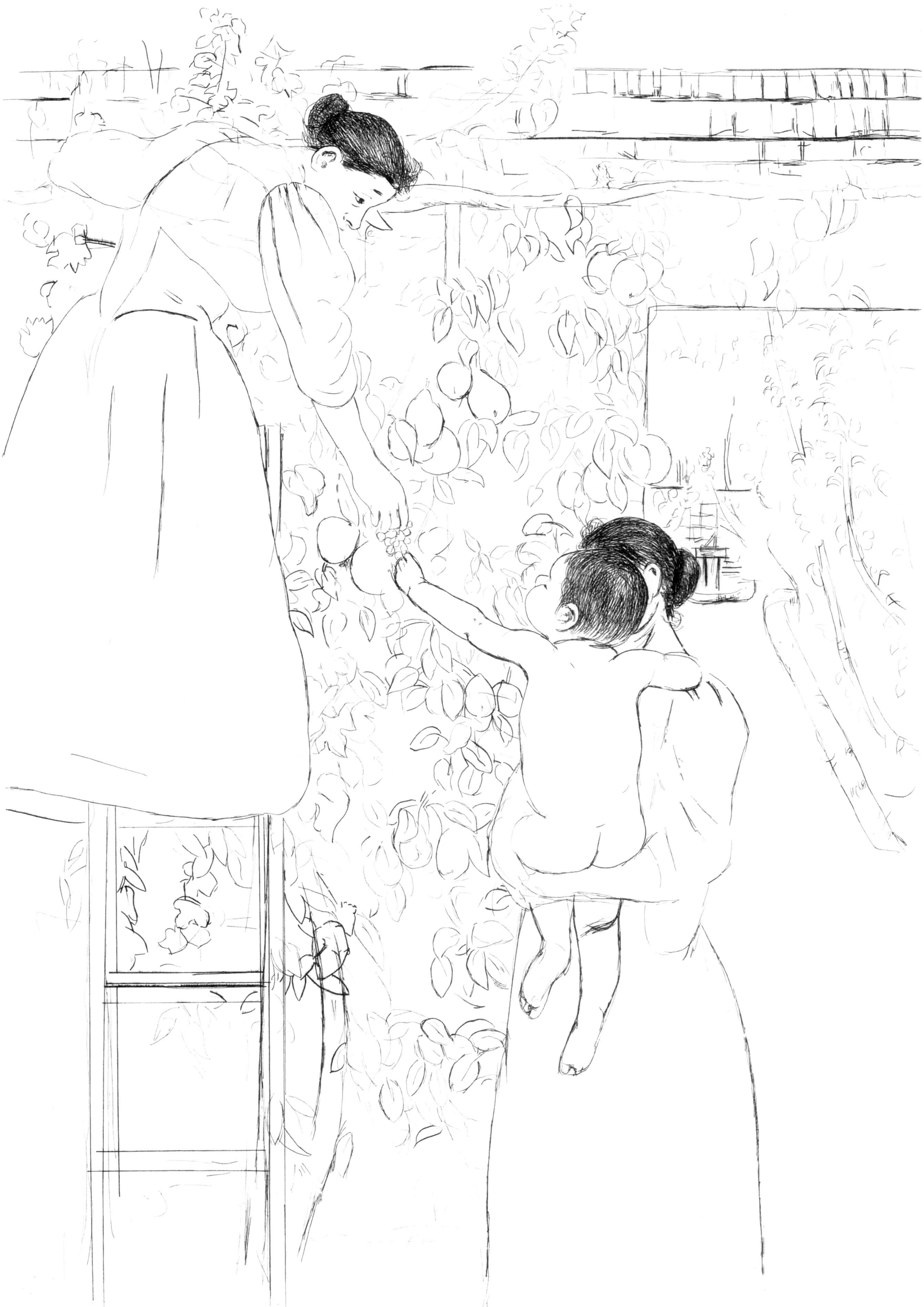

# MARY CASSATT

1844–1926

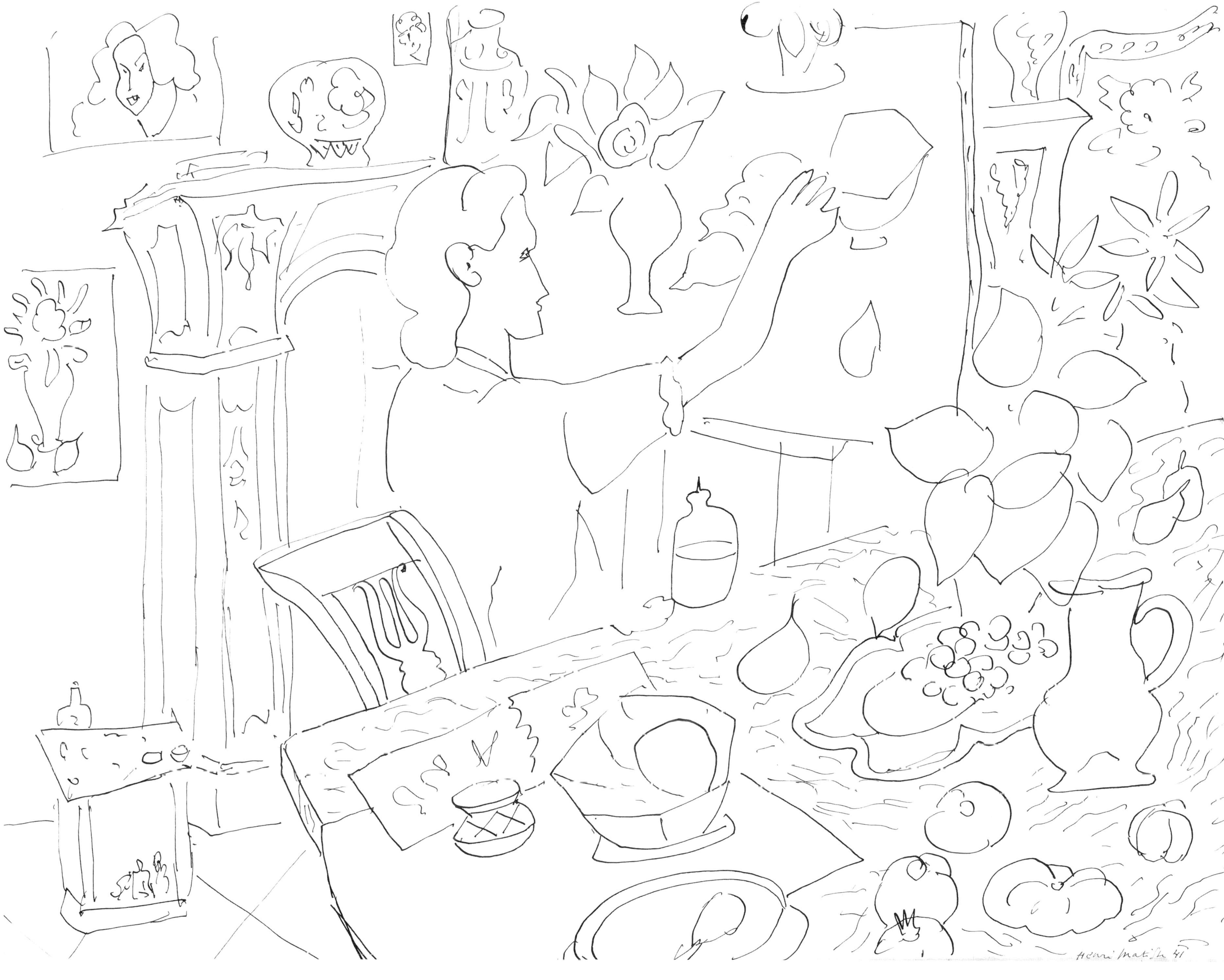
Henri Matisse 41

# HENRI MATISSE

1869–1954

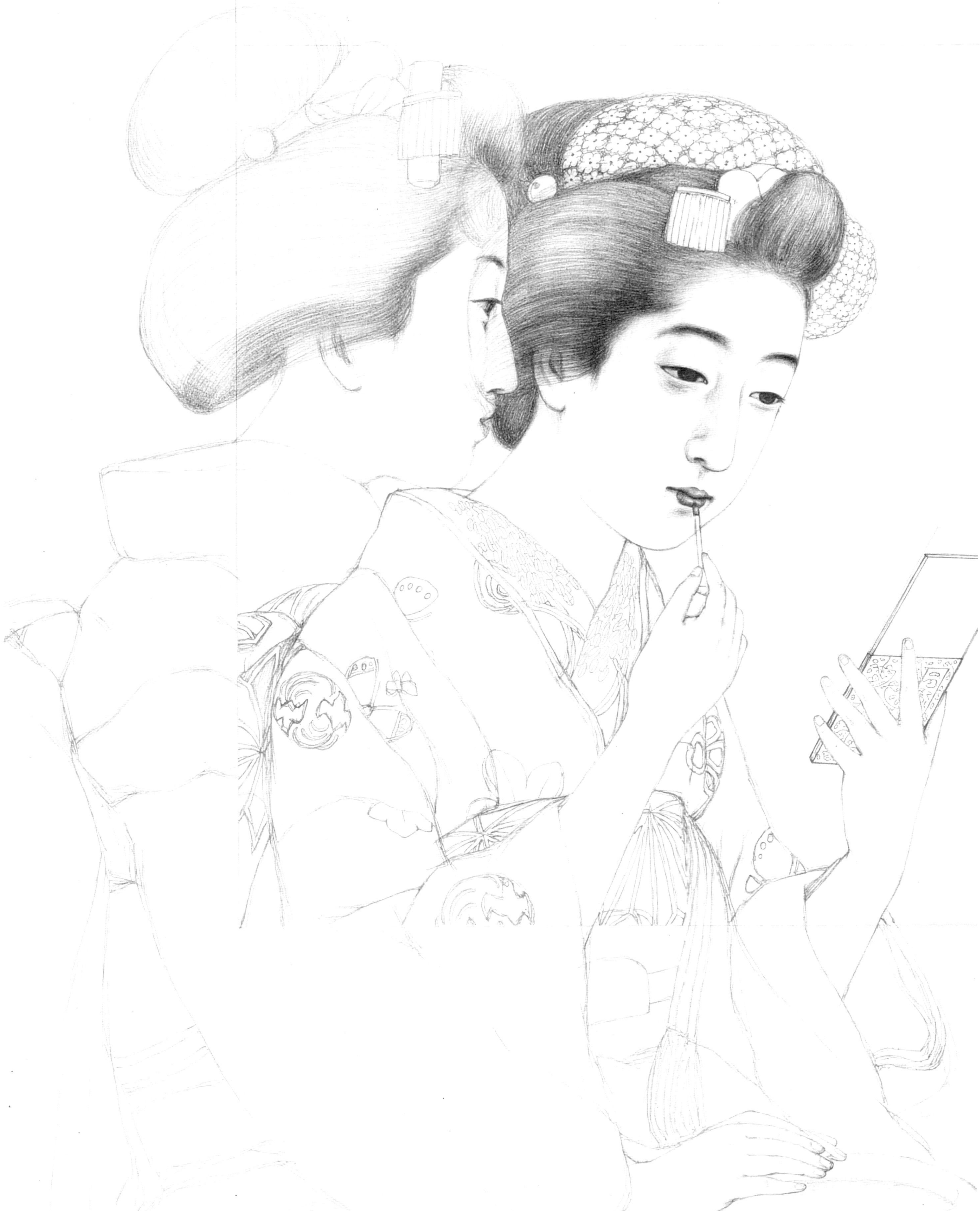

# GOYŌ HASHIGUCHI

1880–1921